The Power
of Your
Subconscious
Mind and
How to Use It

The Master Class Series

~

Awakened Mind

Miracle: The Ideas of Neville Goddard

The Mastery of Good Luck

*The Power of Your Subconscious Mind
and How to Use It*

The Science of Getting Rich Action Plan

Think Your Way to Wealth Action Plan

The Power of Your Subconscious Mind and How to Use It

A MASTER CLASS COURSE WITH

Mitch Horowitz

MEDIA

Published 2020 by Gildan Media LLC
aka G&D Media
www.GandDmedia.com

FIRST EDITION 2020

Cover design by Tom McKeveny

Interior design by Meghan Day Healey of Story Horse, LLC

Library of Congress Cataloging-in-Publication Data is available upon request

ISBN: 978-1-7225-0172-3

10   9   8   7   6   5   4   3   2   1

To the memory of
Thomas Flynn (1966-2020),
who taught that the greatest power
is how you treat another.

Contents

Preface

Of the various Master Classes I have published with G&D Media this one is my personal favorite. This five-part course allows me to explore with you the enduring relevance of Joseph Murphy's ideas and to reexamine them in light of intervening circumstances and complexities of 21st century life. Truths are universal—but they also require reinterpretation by each generation.

This book provides me with a special opportunity to respond to reader letters sent to Joseph Murphy after his death in 1981. While I was researching his life, I discovered a cache of these letters in the files of one his of publishers. It was heartbreaking to read these earnest, handwritten pleas to a man no longer living. You will find a selection of these letters in the afterword, along my own responses. Since human needs are universal, I believe that my personal replies speak to everyone's situation. You will see that these reader letters cover the globe, from Nigeria to Sweden. This gives you a sense not only of Murphy's authorial reach but also of the commonality of all seekers.

In order to benefit from *The Power of Your Subconscious Mind* and Murphy's other works it is unnecessary to agree with his every concept or rationale. I do not. Being a seeker does not entail being a follower. We are here to experiment with and prove ideas in our own lives—not to accept or enforce anything, including what I write in this book.

My greatest hope is that these five lessons stimulate your own thoughts and experiments. *The Power of Your Subconscious Mind* is a book of universal truth primarily because it is *your book*—it is a workshop of practical experimentation, which I beckon you to enter, build within, and then bring your results into the world.

—Mitch Horowitz

CHAPTER ONE

Joseph Murphy, Pioneer of the Subconscious

Literally millions of readers in different languages around the world have read Joseph Murphy's *The Power of Your Subconscious Mind*. When I meet people who are interested in New Thought or mind metaphysics, they often tell me that Murphy's book is their lifelong favorite. People not only read it, but annotate, underline, and reread it. Each time you return to the book it proves a treasure of fresh ideas to help you harness the metaphysical forces of thought. Personally, I've been reading and rereading Murphy's book for years.

Since its publication in 1963, *The Power of Your Subconscious Mind* has taken its place alongside other 20th century mind-power classics including *Think and Grow Rich*, *The Science of Mind*, and *The Game of Life and How to Play it*. But these books do not belong to just one time period. Each generation must reinterpret the greats of practical metaphysics to suit its own needs and outlook. That is the purpose of this Master Class.

The Power of Your Subconscious Mind remains as relevant today as when Murphy wrote it; but there have been intervening developments in science, psychology, domestic life, finance, and the ever-expanding experience of seekers, all of which require contemporary readers to revisit Murphy's work in a manner that is faithful to the original but addresses the challenges we face today.

As a historian and seeker, I have my own theories and interpretations of what is occurring when thought concretizes into reality, and also about the extent and limits of thought force in our physical sphere. In this five-chapter Master Class, I share those insights along with augmentative methods and techniques to attempt.

I want to open this course by exploring the background of the author himself. Murphy and all the figures who attained greatness in the field of mind metaphysics wrote their books with the pen of their own lives. More than anything else, the outlook of New Thought resulted from biography. Every enduring book of mind metaphysics is the testimony of a seeker who discovered something workable in his experience and felt a burning passion to share it. Like many of you reading these words, their experiments and insights led them to feel that they discovered a set of universal, workable principles.

Hence, it is important tell you something about Joseph Murphy the man. Allowing for differences in time, geography, and custom, you may discover that his story mirrors your own.

Murphy was born in 1898 on the southern coast of Ireland to a large Catholic family. He grew up in a devout home and, at his family's urging, planned to study for the priesthood. He entered seminary but left after a single year.

The young seeker rejected the doctrine of no salvation outside the church. Moreover, he believed that the ideas he encountered in seminary did not allow for truths he detected in other faiths. Murphy felt that his views on God, the power of imagination, and the extra-physical nature of thought were neither validated nor given room for exploration.

He went on to study chemistry, eager to learn about the natural laws of life and the principles of cause and effect. Just as combinations across the periodic table produce definite outcomes, Murphy came to believe that the application of spiritual and psychological principles should produce lawful and repeatable results. Since physical elements obey discernable laws, so should spiritual truths operate according to definite principles.

During World War I, Murphy served as a pharmacist in the British medical corps, making use of his chemistry training. After the war he found few opportunities to earn a living as a pharmacist in Dublin's strained economy. So, like many young people of the time, Murphy migrated to America. He was 24 and married to a woman eight years his senior.

In New York City, Murphy found work as a pharmacist. He maintained a pharmacy counter at the famous Algonquin Hotel in Midtown Manhattan, and he also served for several years as a pharmacist with the New York State National Guard. Even as he was busy with his career he developed an increasing interest in the New Metaphysics sweeping the western world: Christian Science, Divine Science, Unity, and Science of Mind.

During the 1930s, Murphy's dedication to these philosophies grew. He became ordained as a Divine Science minister, and began to cultivate his own outlook about the ultimate power of thought.

Murphy was not entirely self-educated. Toward the end of his life, he gave a rare series of interviews to a metaphysical student from Montreal who visited him in Laguna Hills, California, where Murphy was living in a retirement community with his second wife. In these interviews, which appeared only in French, Murphy said that while he was still a young man in New York in the 1930s, he found his way to same mysterious teacher who had mentored another young seeker and migrant with metaphysical ideas: Neville Goddard (1905–1972). Neville, who wrote and spoke under his first name, journeyed from Barbados to New York at age 17 to study theater. Like Murphy, the actor-dancer took a radically different path from what he had planned.

Neville said that his spiritual instructor was a turbaned black man of Jewish decent named Abdullah, who tutored him in mind metaphysics, scripture, Kabbalah, and number symbolism. Murphy, towards the end of his life, said that he had the same teacher. Both young immigrants went on to become leading metaphysical voices of the last century.

There is a strange symmetry to it: these two self-educated men, one from British Barbados, another from the southern coast of Ireland, finding themselves in New York City in the 1930s, one pursuing theater and another making a life for himself as a pharmacist, and each comes to believe in his own way that the golden key to life resides in the own imagination. According to Murphy, both students found their way to the same teacher, Abdullah—and off they went into the world, each to enunciate his vision.

By late 1930s, Murphy, like Neville, began delivering metaphysical lectures and issuing pamphlets on how to use the powers of thought. In later years, one of Murphy's most popular works was *How to Attract Money*, a short book from 1955. Its title highlights Murphy's appeal. The minister had an epic metaphysical vision yet he met people right where they lived, dealing head-on with issues of money, marriage, intimacy, health, and one's wish to grow and to expand in the world.

But it wasn't until 1963, when Murphy was 65, that he broke through to a national audience. That year he published *The Power of your Subconscious Mind*. The book grew enormously popular and has remained so for decades, to the point where, as I mentioned, it is a favorite among many followers of mind metaphysics today.

*   *   *

What was it about *The Power of your Subconscious Mind* that proved so appealing? I think it was the author's ability to combine metaphysics with psychology.

In 1963, concepts of the subconscious were still relatively new to general readers. Even though such ideas had been around for decades, many people still considered the subconscious a fresh and exciting subject. When Rhonda Byrne's *The Secret* first appeared in 2006, I recall colleagues in the New Thought world saying, "Why is this considered a 'secret?' This stuff has been around for more than a century." Therein lies a lesson: subcultures often develop the misimpression that their ideas are better known than they actually are. Byrne grasped that if this material was new to her, it must be to others. She was right. Hence, when Murphy shared his metaphysical perspective on the subconscious mind, he too was breaking new ground for a generation of readers.

The premise of traditional psychology is that you can locate antecedents for problems or neuroses by peeling back the layers of your subconscious. Earlier generations believed that childhood traumas or conditioning become lodged as assumptions within the subliminal or interior mind—and by journeying into your subconscious, using dreams, hypnosis or analysis, you can discover and untangle the knots that cause low self-image or unwanted behavioral patterns. Nowadays we think less in terms of analysis and more in terms of cognitive and behavioral therapy. Nonetheless, the traditional perspective remains powerful.

Murphy honored the premise of traditional psychology, but he expanded it in spiritual directions. Murphy contended that your interior mind is far more than a repository of memories and assumptions. He considered the subconscious an engine of metaphysical expression. As such, it shapes everything that happens to you, from physical wellness to the nature of your relationships to your ability to live out your wishes and intentions in life.

Murphy contended that creation stems from a great higher mind, which is called God in Scripture. He updated an idea that existed among the Ancient Egyptians and Greeks: that all of life is produced by a higher intelligence or over-mind. The Greeks called it *Nous*. Ralph Waldo Emerson called it *The Over-Soul*. Napoleon Hill called it *Infinite Intelligence*. This power courses through you: as you are created in the image of the higher, so do you possess the capacity of creation yourself.

Based on personal observation, Scriptural analysis, and study of the religious traditions of the world, Murphy believed that *the subconscious is the medium of all creation.* In effect, the higher mind uses humanity as its means of expression. You the individual, and specifically your subconscious, is the outlet through which the higher mind functions.

But your subconscious is very vulnerable. It is open to suggestion, good and bad. Since the subconscious is ever operative, you are constantly experiencing the effects of assumptions on which it is fed. Murphy said that the job of your conscious mind is to *protect the subconscious.* The subconscious may be the engine of causation but, like all engines, it requires a filter. You must use your conscious mind to control and shape the suggestions, perceptions, and assumptions that reach your subconscious.

This is why we speak of positive thinking. Positive thinking does not mean going through life with a myopic smile plastered across your face. It is much more powerful than that. It is much more muscular than that. It is not about cultivating a false sense of optimism, suppressing the full range of emotions that you feel, or being disengaged from the events of the world or the challenges facing you or others. Rather, positive thinking means understanding that what you dwell upon in aggregate in your conscious mind, whether action-oriented or desultory, whether productive or dissolute, whether idealistic or cynical, *is going to out picture in your world.*

This is why you must cultivate awareness of what you truly desire in life and whether or how this is being reflected in your thought patterns. Murphy also taught that *desires are sacred.* Desires are a prophetic voice within you, cultivating the actualization of what you need. That doesn't mean taking a hedonistic or go-it-alone approach to life. Murphy also talked about what I call cosmic reciprocity: We are all part of the same circuitry; in order to be generative, sustainably happy, and self-respecting, you must flow through this circuitry in a manner that abets other people's ability to produce and realize their own sense of potential.

Without engaging in the circuitry of benefit, you sink into depression, envy, conflict, and dissatisfaction. Your desires must aid the overall creative process of life or they will prove dissatisfying. Desires are the voice of Infinite Intelligence seeking to reach us. Creation perpetuates itself.

Even after what I've just explained, some people remain concerned about the ethical implications of mind-power philosophy. Some ask,

"What if a dangerous political leader wants to use these methods? Even if such a leader is ultimately defeated, he can still visit mass suffering on the world based upon the power of his subconscious."

Questions of ethics and consequence are universal, regardless of what philosophy we live by. Men and women always face ethical dilemmas. Every day, knowingly or not, we confront such questions, albeit on a smaller scale, when we drive a car, spend with our credit card, get into a conflict, prepare our taxes. Ethical conflicts are a constant. There is always a fork in the road, and there are always unseen consequences.

We more fully appreciate the potential of these consequences by understanding the power of thought. In mind-power philosophy, we are called upon to be even more ethical, even more self-scrutinizing, and hold all the more to a code of reciprocity because the implications of thought are greater than we realize.

Understanding the power of your subconscious gives you an expanded sense of personhood and possibility—and an expanded sense of responsibility. You cannot simply derive your ethics from a book. You cannot be passive. You cannot just say that someone will light the way for you or someone will forgive you. Rather, if you subscribe to Murphy's outlook, it follows that you must cultivate an ethical vision equal to the nature of your nature of your mind.

And remember, even if someone is an ardent materialist—even if he rejects all of the metaphysical ideas that we're exploring here in favor of a strictly physical view of the universe, that person can just as easily abuse power. None of these issues are unique to metaphysics.

Murphy also contends that your subconscious mind will, if allowed, give you discernment. For example, I've spoken of the need for clarified desires. What if you're unsure what your desires are? Or you fear their consequences? Murphy teaches that you can convey your questions or uncertainty to your subconscious, particularly when going to sleep at night, which we will consider in greater detail, and in the same way that your subconscious serves as an outlet of creation, it also serves as an *outlet of ethical clarity.*

Clarity is surprising. As you to come to terms with your true desires and innermost wishes, you may find that they differ from what you began this Master Class believing.

One day I asked a close friend what she wanted out of life. After thinking for a few moments she replied, "I want to be remembered." I liked her statement because it is honest and encompasses a wide range of values. She is an artist; she wants her work to be seen, appreciated, and understood. She wants her work to have integrity and to find posterity. While I counsel specificity in naming your desires, I also believe that you can direct your life in extraordinary ways by *clarifying your values.*

She turned the question back on me: what did I want? Well, I could name my definite chief aim; I could talk about my work as a writer and speaker. But I was inspired by the simplicity and vision of her reply. I told her: "I want to be relevant." Speaking those words for the first time, I suddenly felt very relaxed. I felt good about being able to disclose that.

Within the folds of my desire are also financial wishes, wishes for the quality of my work, and wishes for an audience. But that *one simple statement* served as a clarifying device, mentally and emotionally. It unified my psyche.

What is your highest value in life? Be starkly honest. Sometimes we tell ourselves things that we repeat by rote, without truly examining or re-examining our values. Your needs and wishes may change at different points in life. If you're suffering from an illness or an addiction, your greatest need may be recovery. But several years later, that could change.

What do you want in life? What unifies your psyche? When I say psyche, I mean your intellectual, emotional, and spiritual or extra-physical self. Your psyche is the core of your being.

What value do you most wish to progress towards? This value is not something that necessarily wins the approval of peers or makes you look good to others. The greater likelihood is that others will misunderstand it. Hence, I recommend telling no one outside of a deeply trusted intimate, and even that is optional. I ask only that you be absolutely honest with yourself.

This is a program of action. People sometimes wonder: should I just be thinking about my goal or should I be taking steps toward it? Within the outlook of this class, you are a unified being. There is no division between what is visualized and what is acted upon. If there were, I would call it a false division.

Once you begin to clarify your aims, once you begin to unify your psyche, you will experience flashes of insight, intuition, and directives that will give you *things to do*. If you're not receiving such insights, you may want to re-examine the authenticity of your goal. A goal should be action-oriented. A goal should be something that you can begin to take steps towards, however nascent.

Let's say you wish to become a some kind of medical professional. Do you have the education? Do you have the background? Have you taken the appropriate courses? If not, can you? What educational opportunities are available to you? These questions should be burning within you, and they should be active questions. Otherwise, a goal is fantasy. A true goal, in order to be such, is actionable. There is no division between your mental ideal and that which you act upon.

Joseph Murphy acted with alacrity across the arc of his life. Just a glimpse at the timeline at the back of this book tells you that. He began his career as an intellectually vibrant seeker who studied for the priesthood but didn't find that vessel large enough. So he studied chemistry and sought learn about the natural laws of the universe. He came to feel that not only do these laws function on the elemental scale but they operate on the mental and metaphysical scale, as well. This led Murphy to conclude that psychology, in order to be complete, must recognize that the subconscious is more than a hidden repository of self-image. You are an engine of creation—"as above, so below" goes the Hermetic dictum—and as such your subconscious out-pictures the events and experiences of your life based on the assumptions you feed it.

Murphy *acted* to spread this vision at every stage of his life. Hence, as we conclude this opening lesson I ask you to formulate a simple, brief mission statement: What do you stand for? What do you wish? What do you want to do with your existence? Your subconscious can deliver to you the finest, most effective ways of pursuing and expressing your wish in life, but only if you have clarified it.

I ask you to begin this class with the legitimate hope that you are about to enter a new mindset. During the following chapters, you may undergo a psychological shift as you realize the enormity of your psyche. You are not a toy boat tossed around by tides. You are a creator—in this philosophy you are the medium through which the highest mind creates. I ask you to explore that possibility to its fullest.

CHAPTER TWO

Your Subconscious Mind and Health

All of us in the 21st century recognize a link between psychology and health. We know this from the prevalence of stress-related diseases like hypertension, heart disease, gastric disorders, chromic back and neck pain, and a variety of maladies linked to stress and anxiety.

There exist all kinds of ways that your emotional state impacts your health. But Joseph Murphy threw down a gauntlet. He taught that your health, like all that you experience, is the product of your subconscious, and your subconscious will heal or hurt depending upon the thoughts that populate it—thoughts permitted entry by the gatekeeper of your conscious mind.

This is a contentious issue. It has always been contentious but it is more so today because the health landscape has shifted from Murphy's era. Generally speaking, we experience longer lifespans, which present a complex of eldercare issues. People are capable of living with chronic or debilitating diseases, including Alzheimer's, even as they experience a diminished capacity for life. These problems were not as prevalent in earlier generations when diseases led more quickly to mortality. Today we face new questions.

There are no pat answers about the mind and health, and in this chapter I explore a range of issues, possibilities, and practices.

Many people approach *The Power of Your Subconscious Mind* because they are under duress. They may be experiencing financial problems, directionlessness, health issues or fear of future health issues, especially with the onset of old age.

A few months prior to this writing, I received an email from a woman who works as a registered nurse in Nebraska. She told me that she was reading Joseph Murphy but was having difficulty formulating a sense of purpose. She was a few years away from retirement, she wrote, and worried about impending health and income challenges. Moreover, she didn't feel like there was much room to dream, to expand, or to grow in life. She felt shackled and burdened by her concerns about retirement, although it was also clear from her note that she was preparing for it with financial acumen and responsibility.

I wrote back to her: "You know, in many regards, you have found your aim. You could find a more productive, life-enhancing way of stating that aim, but I think it is this: you are preparing for a happy, sustainable old age. That is your wish. You're still a few years away from retirement. You've been saving, you're an intelligent person, and you have an active, productive profession as a registered nurse. Why not think of saving and planning for potential health needs and other contingencies as a positive goal? Your aim is to have a retirement that isn't marked by financial concerns, that allows you perhaps to travel and engage in leisure, and that is sustained by an appropriate degree of savings and foresight so that your retirement years are happy. That's an admirable, actionable goal."

She wrote back quite enthused. She said my response breathed a new sense of energy into her purpose and life direction. Sometimes the thing we need is what we've already been striving towards, but it must be framed differently.

At the same time, her note raised other issues that are implicitly health related. I often hear from people who have health concerns. A young woman wrote me a few years ago: "I've been researching and reading your ideas about mind metaphysics, and I'm wondering if you specifically have anything that you could recommend for someone with a spinal-cord related injury?" I wrote back the following and I would the same to a member of my own family: "We must treat matters of health as the product of a complexity of causes. I absolutely believe that prayer, meditation, affirmation, and the cultivation of hopeful expectancy play a substantial role in health and recovery. But none of that excludes *availing yourself of the very best in medicine.* We live under many laws and forces. Pursue every viable solution, sometimes simultaneously." I would never give someone a sketchy, rote principle that your health problems are entirely related to your state of mind. I do not believe that's the point we should be taking from mind-power literature.

Murphy never discouraged seeking medical care. Although he did contend that the only reason certain treatments or medicines work is because the individual believes in their effectiveness. Belief impacts the effectiveness of treatment, as we'll explore. But I do not consider belief the only factor at work. Nor are the results of belief always predictable. A universal principle or law can function differently at different times. Take the law of gravity, for example. Gravity is ever operative; but you are going to experience gravity differently on earth than on Jupiter or in the vacuum of space. This is because gravity responds to mass. In a certain sense, gravity is mass being attracted to itself. In the vacuum of space, where there is no mass, there are no effects from gravity. If you introduce mass in ever-greater increments the effects of gravity will be increasingly felt.

I believe that something like this goes on with the law of mentality. I agree with Murphy that our minds are conduits of higher intelligence. Seen differently, it is possible that our perspective can *select* experiences from among infinite possibilities, a theory I explore in *The Miracle Club*. But I also believe that within this physical sphere we do not necessarily experience the principle of mind causation consistently because laws are affected by myriad factors.

If you're in recovery, if you're convalescing, if you're experiencing an illness, my wish is that you use this material in conjunction with the best of everything that's available to today, including traditional medical care. Withhold nothing, exclude nothing, and employ all forces.

Physical wellness is necessary to reach your potential. Ralph Waldo Emerson published a wonderful essay in 1860 called "Power," in which he analyzed the ingredients of personal power. He wrote that the foundation of power must be wellness, because if you're suffering from an illness then all of your energies must go towards recovery. Emerson considered wellness a precondition to personal power.

Once that condition is satisfied, Emerson taught, there are two ingredients to exercising power: *concentration* and *drilling*. By concentration, he meant focusing all of your energies on a certain point. That is a law of nature. What occurs in nature and the cosmic order repeats within our psyches. This is another meaning of the Hermetic dictum, "As above, so below." Photons of light may be undetectable, but heavily concentrated they form a laser. You can wave away a trickle of water or current of air—but when these elements are sharply focused they wield tremendous force. The same is true of your psyche. Concentration in the form of a clarified aim, wish, or purpose is *the first ingredient to power.*

The second ingredient is *drilling.* By drilling, Emerson meant repeat actions like rehearsing or training. Once you determine your focus, you train and train and train, like a martial artist, dancer, or athlete. You constantly go through your routine, practice, or craft until it is second nature.

Predicating all this, however, is physical vitality. What role does the mind play in that? I think we are only beginning to understand the consequential nature of outlook and wellness.

Thoughts and feelings of youthfulness can actually strengthen and fortify your body. Harvard psychologist Ellen Langer demonstrated this in an innovative aging study in 1981. Langer assembled elderly subjects from assisted living facilities and placed them into a nostalgic dwelling space intended to evoke feelings of youth. She surrounded them with music, movies, and other media associated with their youth. Appliances, furniture, reading material, and the general setting likewise evoked their earlier years. After several weeks the subjects overall tested for improved physical traits. Blood pressure dropped, muscle mass improved, muscle to body fat ratios improved, and even eyesight improved. Feelings of depression or anxiety eased or lifted. The very fact of placing people into settings that made them feel young seemed to reverse certain markers of age-related decline. Since experiments like this are necessarily limited in time frame they leave open the question of novelty. Novelty is an important factor in mood, such as the uplift you experience when travelling to new places. Sustaining novelty and engagement may be a factor in long-term benefits.

Although we do not fully understand the delivery mechanism or all the ancillary factors, belief, attitude, engagement, and emotion wield measurable influence over age-related decline. Sustained thoughts not only affect bodily functioning but also the structural makeup of the brain. Research from the field of neuroplasticity demonstrates that repetitive thought patterns alter the pathways through which electrical impulses travel in the brain. In short, thought changes brain biology.

In a series of studies beginning in the 1990s, UCLA research psychiatrist Jeffrey M. Schwartz demonstrated the impact of thoughts on gray matter. Through behavioral treatment programs and comparative brain scans, Schwartz determined that if subjects suffering from addictions or obsessive-compulsive disorder sustainably redirected their thoughts away from undesired behaviors, the neural pathways by which electrical impulses travel actually alter. No one challenges the validity of this data. But very few observers are willing to face its implications. Schwartz and his colleagues demonstrated—and he acknowledges this forthrightly—the existence of mind over matter.

Neuroplasticity upends everything we are raised to believe. We are traditionally taught that the brain produces thoughts; thoughts don't produce or alter brain matter. Yet Schwartz demonstrated that thoughts alter neural pathways. How can we say that thought doesn't evince a force? How can anyone today seriously argue that materialism covers all the bases of life? Materialists contend that thought is an epiphenomenon of the brain, and once the brain is gone, thought too vanishes in the same way that the bubbles vanish from a glass of carbonated water. It simply doesn't work that way. The materialist paradigm no longer covers the observable circumstances of life.

Joseph Murphy and other New Thought pioneers had a sharp instinct for this truth, sometimes going back to the early 20th century. Generations later neuroscience reached supporting conclusions, although rarely with knowledge of the preceding insights.

I noted that Murphy wrote that how you feel about a treatment or medication is the determining factor as to whether it is effective. Let's consider that claim in light of recent placebo studies.

In January of 2014, a team of researchers at Harvard Medical School published an unprecedented placebo study using an active drug, in this case a migraine medication. Placebo studies typically use an inert substance, like a sugar pill. But in this case researchers wanted to test the impact of patients receiving positive information about an active substance. Would this information alter their experience?

Two groups of patients received the same migraine meditation. The control group knew it was being given a migraine drug, and that was that. The other group was given the same drug, along with positive and accurate information about its benefits. Researchers found that among the group receiving positive information, the reported effectiveness of the drug was higher. Patients did better with the prescription when they experienced positive expectancy. The study demonstrates that the placebo effect is *ever operative*; it does not just kick in when we're given a false expectancy and an inert substance. Rather the placebo response enhances our experiences, for good or ill, whenever we're receiving treatment.

These findings not only support Murphy's observation but they bear out the insight of another mind-power pioneer Emile Coué

(1857–1926). Coué was a French mind theorist who famously prescribed the mantra, "Day by day, in every way, I am getting better and better." Before becoming famous for his mantra (which we will revisit), Coué worked as a druggist in the early 1900s in the town of Troyes in northwestern France. He noticed that his clients seemed to do better with medications when he spoke in praise of a certain formula. Coué documented this experience.

In 2014—more than a century later—Harvard's researchers reached the same conclusion. I asked the researchers whether they were thinking of Coué when they structured the study. Ted Kaptchuk, the head of Harvard's program in placebo studies, told me they were not, but acknowledged that their findings comported with Coué's. Much of what's occurring in placebo studies echoes the insights of early New Thoughters.

Other studies demonstrate that the placebo effect works even when patients *know* they are receiving a sham pill. A 2010 Harvard study documented the benefits of a so-called transparent placebo. In this experiment, a group of subjects suffering from irritable bowel syndrome were told that they were receiving a placebo. They knew they were receiving a "nothing pill." Nonetheless, 59 percent of sufferers who took the "honest placebo" reported relief (compared to 35 percent in the control group). This suggests people's general belief in the efficacy of placebos, which in itself was sufficient to trigger a healthful response.

Even after a near-century of study, we do not fully know what's going on with the placebo effect. We use the term "placebo" so often that we think we understand what's happening simply because we can put a name on it. Some clinicians theorize that the placebo effect is the release of endorphins or pain-relieving enzymes into the bloodstream. That may be one of a variety of factors; but because we've identified one piece of a puzzle does not mean we've got the whole picture. One could even say that endorphin-release is what the moral or religious appeal looks like in the body. Yet there exist a wide range of recorded placebo responses that go far beyond these implications.

The aforementioned researcher Ellen Langer constructed another fascinating study about how perception impacts physiology. In 2007, Langer assembled a group of subjects who worked as hotel maids. Most of these women believed they did not get much exercise. Langer knew otherwise. She wanted to test the effects of this knowledge on their bodies. Langer placed one group of maids into a control group, which went about its work as usual. A second group also continued with its work—but with a difference: Langer and her colleagues informed this other group that its daily tasks have definite aerobic and anaerobic benefits, such as the number of calories burned and the raising of heart rate. The maids were on their feet doing all kinds of labor, pushing vacuum cleaners, scrubbing, making beds, and so on. Contrary to their self-perception, they were quite active. Langer and her associates accurately explained this. Within a month the group that received this information experienced weight loss, lowered blood pressure, and improved muscle mass ratios. The other group experienced no change.

Just being accurately informed about the benefits of their physical activity resulted in health improvements, including weight loss.

Why should physical improvements emerge from information alone? No such thing appeared in the control group. Langer found no difference between the routines of the two groups. Nonetheless, perception of physical activity evinced measurable benefits. If you believe you are exercising, your body responds as though you are.

This adds a profound layer of depth to the impact of thought and expectancy, not only as it relates to illness but to overall vitality.

*   *   *

The Power of your Subconscious Mind is filled with affirmations, prayers, and visualizations that can be used in pursuit of health. I want to add a further dimension to that approach. Based on what we have been considering, it is profoundly important to stay in touch with things that you found motivating, exciting, and arousing when you were young.

As discussed, such things have a positive impact on vigor and youth-related physical traits. I am 54 years old as I'm writing these words. You can make up your own mind about this, and I'm not pushing one point of view or another, but most people express surprise when they learn my age. I practice all the ordinary things that we've been taught as far as health is concerned. But I believe that my passion for the material I work with—the very things you and I are now considering—plays a tremendous role in my bodily vitality.

I stay in touch with things that brought me joy when I was younger: music, imagery, design, style—things that I love. I believe it is more important than you may realize to cultivate a self-image that makes you feel vibrant. I enjoy getting tattoos. I enjoy music. I enjoy the people I circulate among. I seek out company that feeds me rather than depletes me. I will not tolerate the later. As much as possible, I live in and visit places that help me feel a sense of excitement and meaning. Are these things the metaphorical fountain of youth? Well in a certain sense, yes.

I believe that we give into physical decline much too easily, and much sooner than we are required to.

Take personal cues from the studies we've been reviewing. Take account of everything that you are doing in life and the ways in which it can contribute to your wellbeing and vitality. Awareness, perception, and understanding are critical forces in maintaining wellness, and not just when you are ill.

One of the most neglected keys to that greater vitality is *placing yourself in circumstances, among company, and into activities that give you feelings of arousal, happiness, discovery, and excitement.* Those are elixirs of life.

We experience sharp limits in this physical sphere. If you kick a stone, you are going to experience pain. There is no viable exception. That is an experience under which we must live in this sphere of existence. Are there other spheres of existence? I believe so. This is supported by facts of extra-physicality, which we can infer from psychical research, quantum theory, neuroplasticity, and testimony from seekers across generations.

I believe there are spheres beyond the one that we experience. Murphy taught that we are expressions of higher mind and, as such, are part of eternity. In death, he taught, we reenter the universal mind. We reintegrate into the source of energy from which all life emerges. Hence, we are always part of the wellspring of creation.

But it is important to clarify what this means apropos of eternal recurrence or reincarnation. In the modern West, we tend to view reincarnation as the recurrence of distinct personas. The concept is that we crossover into death and then reenter physical life maybe with different traits, but carrying some kind of karma and perhaps personality ticks or physical markings from previous incarnations. That, more or less, is the modern Western view.

But Murphy's perspective differs from most modern concepts of reincarnation. His idea of eternal recurrence comports with some of the earliest concepts of reincarnation from ancient Vedic teachings. Vedic philosophy teaches that every source of individual life reenters the energy of creation after death, and then returns to the physical realm, *but not necessarily as distinctly related to a previous incarnation.* Rather, life energy is continually reintegrated into different forms after the individual reenters infinite mind. Life is ineffable and eternal; but that energy, as it returns to our sphere, does not necessarily reflect or bear the markings of previous or accumulated incarnations.

Likewise, in Murphy's view we live forever—but as a collective energetic field not as individual personas.*

---

* You can read further about this in Murphy's 1954 book, *The Meaning of Reincarnation*, reprinted in *The Wisdom of Joseph Murphy* (G&D Media, 2020).

CHAPTER THREE

Your Subconscious Mind and Success

We have considered that your conscious mind functions as a gatekeeper for your subconscious. The ideas, images, and emotional responses that reach your subconscious, and reach it with some degree of consistency, outpicture in your life. This effect is perpetually at work. The question is how to use it.

One of the stumbling blocks we encounter when harnessing the powers of the mind—and Murphy wrote frequently about this—is that we fixate on *one absolute outcome*.

If we want a relationship, or if we want marriage, we tend to fixate on one individual whom we believe is going to bring us happiness. If we're looking for some kind of break-through in our work, we often think in terms of one royal road to success. Murphy called this a mistake. I have lived out this error several times. For example, when I make an inquiry to someone, I usually make it with the wish that they're going to respond in kind. If I don't hear back, or if I hear back belatedly, I get squirrely about whether the other party is receptive. (You may wonder at my self-disclosure. It is purposeful. I do not believe that the pioneers of positive thinking were sufficiently disclosing of their own frailties. I want to overturn that practice.) When I return to *The Power of your Subconscious Mind*, however, I am refreshed. I am reminded that *good never comes from just one place.* The Jewish sage Menachem Schneer-son (1902–1994) observed, "Good things always arrive unexpectedly."

I do believe that we experience moments of higher perspective. But when we are under stress, fear, or in a state of unsatisfied desire, our perspective gets lost. I can tell you of numer-ous occasions, professionally and personally, where I have wished for the right answer from the right person only to discover, in using the powers of my mind more flexibly, the answer arrived from an entirely different and better place. I want to give you a personal example.

For almost thirty years I worked in book publishing. For the latter part of my career, I was an executive at Penguin Random House. Later in my career, I developed a strong interest in narrating audio books, and I found success in doing this. I worked on books that performed well. The engineers and producers were happy. During this time there was an out-of-print self-help book I wanted to republish. I worked hard to secure the licensing rights. It was an old classic by a long-dead author and I had to track down her surviving relatives in New England.

That done, I told an audio publisher with whom I had worked previously, and with whom I had a good relationship, that I wanted narrate this book. I heard nothing back, dead silence. I inquired again, still silence. Finally, she came back to me, and said no. No particular reason was given, and that was that. I felt left out in the cold because I had worked hard to secure rights for this book and I had distinguished myself as a capable narrator.

Rather than go to a place of resentment or confusion, although I felt some of both, I instead went into a place of mental visualization. I pictured myself recording this book, and lots more besides, and receiving industry recognition for it. I spent about two weeks picturing, visualizing, and adopting the feeling state of this outcome. I took no outer action.

To my delight and surprise, I heard from a rights manager that *another* audio publisher wanted to acquire audio rights to this book. Would it be okay to move it, she asked, because they were making a robust offer and no agreement had been reached with the other audio house. I said yes. I also asked if the rights manager would tell them I'd like to narrate the book. She agreed. This rights manager came back to me almost immediately and said, "I told them and they said that they've been emailing you about your narrating books for them and you haven't responded." I had received no such emails.

I went into my junk-mail filter; nothing was there. I then went into a still-deeper layer of spam filter—and there was a week-old message inviting me to narrate for them and saying that they wanted me to narrate not just one but two books. They ended up adding this third book to the deal. I formed a tight relationship with that audio publisher. They are responsible for the very book you're reading now.

This episode began with an apparent failure. But it wasn't failure. What I needed was in a different direction from the one I had selected.

Now, I do not believe that we always lack perspective. At special moments we do have perspective on our highest good. This occurs when habitual or rote thoughts get interrupted. This can occur at moments of euphoria or moments of grief. Other times it may occur in deep states of prayer or meditation. Or in dream states. Higher perspective can reach us whenever the gerbil wheel of the mind briefly stops spinning and we're open to other influences. But when stress returns, perspective recedes.

Murphy understood that at stressful periods you must *exit the field of activity* and go within. Undertake this journey with the confidence, resolve, and expectancy that you are going to receive what you need. You may receive it in a vastly better and more sustainable manner than whatever your fixed point of interest is at a limited moment.

This is also true when seeking a mate, partner, or spouse. Murphy's contemporary Neville Goddard told a story that bears on this. Neville recalled that students often approached him with the wish to marry a certain man or woman. Neville would remind them, "You don't know that that's the one. Your imagination will bring you what you need. Don't paint yourself into a corner. Don't persuade yourself that it's him or nothing." And Neville recalled that students would almost invariably respond, "Oh no, I am certain. It must be this man." Neville would again smile and say, "Don't convince yourself of that." He advised simply imagining that you have found the right mate.

Time after time, Neville recalled, his students would get married, invite him to the wedding, and he would sit there in the pew watching the bride or groom come down the aisle with someone else.

It is important to clarify your *real needs*—and not to confuse means with ends. You may say that you want a certain job when your actual need is for security. Be certain about the *condition* you need. Not the thing, person, or perceived vehicle.

This phenomenon has saved me in relationships. I once was seeking a partner, and I felt certain that one person was just right. I felt this with such certainty that it was almost palpable. And yet I found that my mental exercises delivered me to a different person—who was exactly the right one. I have witnessed this in my experiences again and again.

Also allow for a time interval. I am doing things today that I dreamed of in my earliest memories around age three or four. And when I make those connections between past and present it is uncanny. It took me years to get here but my life is, in many ways, the mind's eye picture of what I wished for from my earliest years, including my writing these words to you right now.

We sometimes snap to realization of incredible congruity between what we're currently experiencing and our earliest mental images.

I've made several references to visualization. What are the best methods of visualization? The method that I have had the most success with, and that comports with everything Murphy wrote, is to visualize yourself *within* a scene that implies the fulfillment of your wish. Do not watch yourself as though you are looking at a movie screen. See from within the scene itself.

For example, if you want a promotion at work, you might imagine yourself shaking the hand of your boss as he is saying, "Congratulations." That's all—just something very simple. Allow that scene, with you as protagonist, to repeat in your mind as often as it feels natural. Try to experience the emotions of your wish fulfilled.

Run the scene through your head as you're going about your daily routines—but especially as you're drifting to sleep at night and waking in the morning. Sleep researchers call this period *hypnagogia*. It is the borderland between sleep and wakefulness. In the hypnagogic state your mind is uniquely supple, flexible, and suggestible. Your rational defenses are down. Yet you remain conscious and cognizant. Hence, you can direct your thoughts.

During hypnagogia your mental images bend and morph like the scenes in a Salvador Dali painting. Your rational apparatus is down. But you are sufficiently cognizant to select mental pictures or suggestions. And you are less likely to push back against them. You are persuadable.

There's a negative side to this as well. The lowering of your rational defenses during hypnagogia is why anxieties get exaggerated in the pre-dawn hours or during bouts of insomnia. In periods when we drift in and out of sleep we often think about problems with exaggerated severity. It is imperative that you use this period constructively rather than give yourself over to the gremlins of the psyche.

When you visualize, I encourage you to use very simple scenes. This helps keep your attention from wandering. Most people find it easier to remain focused on a small scene rather than a complex one, which brings with it all kinds of mental associations that might distract you. Although if you are able to sustain a more complex scene and remain focused, then by all means do so. The key is consistency and naturalness.

Let's say you want money. You might picture yourself in front of a computer screen looking at your bank balance, seeing a certain number and feeling thrilled. Run that scene through your mind as long as it feels natural. Maybe you want to be married. As we've seen, you don't need to fixate on one partner. Try feeling the ring on your finger. Feel the weight, substance, and solidity of a wedding band. Turn this band around on your finger, not physically, but in your mental picture. Maybe there's somewhere you wish to live, maybe a warm weather environment. Picture yourself behind the wheel of a car or in the passenger seat reaching your home or workplace in this beautiful, warm environment with a gentle breeze blowing into the car; see sunshine or palm trees out the window; smell the sea air. You might be passing over a bridge where you feel a warm breeze coming off the bay. Keep it simple and evocative. The mind creates in a state of sensory experience.

Likewise, the mind responds to emotions. You might puzzle over why you vividly remember something from childhood that a sibling does not. This is because *emotions form memories*. If someone doesn't ascribe the same emotional importance to an event, he or she may not recall it. Emotions, whether positive or negative, signal to us what is important. That is why positive emotions should always be heeded because they are pointing towards something that truly matters. Feelings are the key to your inner self.

We talk of positive thinking, but that's a little misleading because thought and emotion are different. The mind runs on its own track, emotions on their own track, and the body on its own track. That's why, for example, we might make a mental vow not to get angry in a given situation. But something triggers us, emotions rise, and anger erupts. Or you might make a vow that you're not going to eat past a certain hour; but the body is hungry, and next thing you know you're at the refrigerator. If thoughts alone were the engine of creativity, there would be no addictions and no destructive behavioral patterns.

What's important is that your psyche be unified: to enter a state of creativity you must have a mental-emotional experience; and it's easiest to have a mental-emotional experience when you're centered on an evocative picture.

Consider: we use our sense of sight before we can speak. We use speech before we can write. We use touch and hearing before almost anything. This is true for the individual and it is true for humanity as a whole. Most of our great stories and myths began as symbol and oral tradition, and only later were written down. I've made reference to Hermeticism. This is a collection of wisdom from Ancient Egypt that was later set down in standard expository form by Greek writers in the generations following Christ. These ideas had previously existed for centuries in symbolic and oral form. Picture and speech are our primary means of communication. In the infant, sight and speech develop first. Hence, your most natural form of communicating with your psyche is through emotionalized scenes.

To recap, think of a very simple scene that implies the fulfillment of your desire. Don't look at that scene as if you're passively sitting outside of it, as if watching yourself on a screen, but be in it, feel yourself in it. You are the protagonist. What are you experiencing? Is it a handshake? Is it a ring on your finger? Is it sunshine on your face? Is it your arrival at a destination that implies your success?

Allow that scene to run through your mind as long as it feels natural. The story I told earlier about the audiobook took me about two weeks. Other times it has taken me years. In some regards, you could say that it has taken me a lifetime. But I have gotten where I wish to be. I wish the same for you.

CHAPTER FOUR

Overcoming Mental Blocks

I believe that most of us possess immensely greater abilities and inner reserves than we realize. Yet we get stuck. We do not always act in the world as we are truly capable of acting. There are moments when we all feel that we could be an A-student, that we could get a promotion in rank or career, that we could complete a work of art or academic project, if only . . . If only what? What is going on when we experience "if only?" Too often we live from a glacially marginal place. We're living from that portion of the ice glacier that peaks above the surface, just as our psyche peaks into daily life; yet below the surface exists a greater and more potent self.

A plus-entity dwells within all of us. Yet we rarely access it. This is sometimes due to feelings of chronic inferiority, which have gripped us since childhood. This problem can arise from a mysterious interplay of nature and conditioning. We are all born with a fixed temperament or character. I vividly recall my two sons coming from the womb with discernable personality traits. Today, they are adolescents and the same personality traits prevail. I believe this is true for all of us. At the same time, those innate traits interplay with environmental conditioning. This arguably makes conditioning all the more important because whatever in us is strong and adaptable or weak and rigid gets accentuated by conditioning. The manner in which those attributes intermingle with environment determines our self-image.

Self-image can feel so concrete, and it gets so continually reinforced by perception, that it seems like a physical organ or limb. It seems fixed, organic, and palpable. But self-image *can be changed*. That change may take a lifetime, as it has for me, or a shift can occur quickly, sometimes in the form of an epiphany. There is no single manner that works for all of us. But we all experience similar limitations stemming from self-image. If untreated, these limitations form mental blocks that limit your sense of ability.

The philosopher Cardi B observed that if you want money you must ask for it. You must plainly step forward and state what you require. She's wiser than I was at her age. And she's absolutely right—but mental blocks get in our way. Hence, we are often incapable of asking for what we want, from others and ourselves.

Of course, there's an important adjunct to asking for what we want. We must also deliver what others need. Mental blocks not only cause low self-assessment but trigger fear, which results in procrastination and self-sabotage. Mental blocks prevent people from keeping their word, from following through, from delivering the kind of excellent work for which they expect to be paid. Hence, this chapter is dedicated to overcoming mental blocks.

Years ago a spiritual teacher told me, "You do everything with your heart. So how do you get anything done when your heart's not in it?" His observation was dead on. If you give me a task or issue me a challenge, and it really engages me, almost nothing, save for radically unforeseen circumstances, will stop me. I dedicate myself to everything I write, to every talk, to every narration. But when I am pressed into doing something that I do not want to, I feel indifferent.

At times, all of us must do things that we would rather not. Yet sometimes an unwanted task may not actually be necessary. We occasionally (or even frequently) accept tasks without considering whether we really must. Allow yourself the freedom to ask whether a given task is something that you want to do, or need to do. When possible, I advise working only on things that your heart is in. You will find it much easier to summon your energies.

Let's say that you sincerely want to engage in a task but feel internally blocked. You cannot get started. That is often fear. In that vein, I want to share a piece of wisdom from a self-help book written in 1936 called *Wake Up and Live!* by Dorothea Brande. Brande provided a powerful, simple principle of achievement. It is so simple that we are apt to wave it off. But if you act on it you will discover new dimensions within yourself. First let me supply a bit of background, so that you can fully appreciate Brande's advice.

Brande argued that most of us have a *will to fail*. She contended that we fear humiliation more than we are desire success. We are so afraid to fumble the ball that we disengage; we either move out of the way of the ball or drop it preemptively.

I know capable people who constantly blow deadlines, break their word, procrastinate, or demonstrate some weird unaccountability almost ensuring failure. This is self-sabotage. The individual is so lacking a sense of confidence in his own abilities and is so frightened of humiliation that he averts the prospect by rushing toward the losers' corner, by stumbling and never making an effort to complete the race. This is an aversion to imagined pain. It is a will to fail

One of the most difficult things about dealing with anxiety is that what you fear is almost always projected into an imagined future. Hence, the anxious person is locked into a pattern of anticipatory anxiety. To avert the phantom tragedy he takes himself out of the running. He makes failure a fait accompli.

Brande offered a simple solution: *Act as though it is impossible to fail.* That's it. Act as though it is impossible to fail. If you live by that principle you will discover success at unexpected hours and across a vast range of undertakings. This is because her principle averts the fear-based, imagination-based *will to fail*.

If you run toward the ball rather than away from it, if you *want* the ball to come to you rather than hoping it goes to next person, if you act contrary to your fear impulses, you go a long way toward surmounting mental blocks. You also enlist the powers of your sub-conscious *because action implies fulfillment.*

Philosopher William James (1842–1910) observed that nothing is actually possible unless you are willing to take a risk on the *maybe*: maybe I can do it, maybe I can succeed. If it weren't for the self-possession that implies the ability to do something, you would take no chances at all. Critics of positive thinking rarely understand this.

As an example, James said to imagine that you are mountain climbing, and you must, as a mortal necessity, leap over an abyss or a chasm. Your willingness to take a chance on the *maybe*, to take a chance on making it, is the only factor that allows for the possibility of success. Usually the better part of risk is taking it, provided the aim is a necessity or at least would make a great deal of positive dif-ference.

Brande made the same point. The mental or physical act, which is not usually one of life or death, must be undertaken as though it is impossible to fail. You must act with agency to achieve what is possible. I promise you that what is possible is probably greater and fuller than what you've imagined. And the risk is less.

But you will be unable to verify this unless you act as though it is impossible to fail.

There is another and more difficult class of mental block. This block appears in people who perpetually fail to display accountability. They leave tasks half done. They agree to help and do not deliver. They overlook or ignore details. That kind of mental block is graver than the ones I've been describing because it is easier to conceal, including from yourself.

In my experience, a disproportionate number of people with such blocks are found within the New Age or alternative spiritual culture. I want to be clear that I use the term New Age in a positive way. My definition of New Age is therapeutic spirituality. I love New Age culture. But over the course of decades I have encountered a large fraction of people within New Age culture whose chief flaw is *lack of accountability*. In some cases, such people are fleeing from their inability or self-perceived inability to get things done in outer life. Rather than confronting that issue, they hide from it by claiming to live from a scale of "spiritual" values or from being "laid back." But we can never flee from ourselves. James Allen wrote in 1909, "He who lacks thoroughness in his worldly duties, will also lack the same quality in spiritual things."

I sometimes encountered this attitude in book publishing. I witnessed editorial and publicity assistants who seemed constitutionally averse to applying themselves to necessary tasks. Writers would contact me—including some good colleagues who I knew were reluctant to complain—to say that a pertinent question was ignored, a package never arrived, or a book never sent to an eager reviewer.

On a related note, I could tell almost immediately from the condition in which an author's manuscript arrived whether it was going to be a good read: is there a proper title page, is there a table of contents, are there well-organized footnotes, are the pages numbered? (You wouldn't believe how many manuscripts I received where the pages weren't numbered.)

On one occasion I received such a telltale manuscript from a fairly prominent natural health writer. Pages from a different book appeared on the back of each one of his manuscript pages. At first I was perplexed. Then I realized that he had used an old recycled manuscript to print on. Such a move wreaks havoc on the publishing process. Unsurprisingly, the manuscript wasn't much good. A friend has an expression: "The way you do one thing is the way you do everything." If someone ignores a detail, chances are he ignores all details. And if someone is impeccable in one way, chances are he is impeccable in all sorts of ways.

Are you impeccable? Do you give everything your all? What would people around you say? What would your spouse say? What would your kids say? What would your co-workers say? What would your boss say? What would your commanding officer say? Are you the kind of person upon whom others can depend? Are you the kind of person who removes stress from other people's lives or who adds stress to other people's lives?

The degree to which we deliver—or fail to—can expose concealed hostility. An incisive spiritual teacher named Vernon Howard (1918–1992) observed that *what we call ineptitude is often hostility.* This is because ineptitude has the same *effects* as hostility. People are made to feel nervous. People are made to feel unsure. People are left unsteady. People must cover for someone else. People are forced to do additional work. The inept person demands undeserved rewards. Vernon always wanted people to look at effects. Don't look at the explanation, he said, look at the impact.

Sometimes we subtly, even insidiously, withhold our best from the world. The exercises we are exploring will not deliver unless you have come to terms with the *first causes* of your thoughts. This relates to what we considered in chapter one about the importance of a unified psyche. What do you want? Do you want to be an effective person? Or do you want to run and hide? And if you want to run and hide, why? Is it because you harbor a sense of inferiority or fear of failure? Or is it perhaps that you're just with the wrong crowd and you're applying yourself to the wrong tasks?

Perhaps a different environment would make all the difference in your life. Mental blocks can result in self-imposed attachments to the wrong peers. You will sometimes observe a kid who runs with a circle of friends who don't seem very nice to him. Maybe the friends bully or exclude him. He may implicitly feel that he has no choice but to hang around with this group, perhaps because they are just in the neighborhood. But there is a choice. We can almost always select a new environment or social circle, even if we do not physically change locales. Relationships define your environment.

I want to share a story about overcoming perceived limitations. I hope it will help you achieve something practical in your own life. Years ago I was trying to establish my name as a writer in metaphysics. I was writing for a variety of small magazines. I didn't always believe that these magazines were treating my stories with the proper degree of prominence or giving my work sufficient play. While I was working on my first book, *Occult America*, a metaphysical magazine asked me to contribute an article. I offered a piece of my book-in-progress. They excitedly accepted. When the magazine appeared my article was buried deep inside and wasn't treated with any degree of prominence. I felt like my work was undervalued. This was all the more ironic because I believed, as someone dedicated to his craft, that my work was of higher quality than the norm in such places.

A short while later I was having lunch with a friend, Mark Thurston, who is a scholar of metaphysical traditions. I began relating my predicament. Mark made an observation that was simple yet revolutionary. He looked across the table and said, "It sounds like you need to be writing for better magazines." Why did I remain in this limited neighborhood?

I took his advice. In the years immediately ahead I had bylines in *The New York Times*, *The Wall Street Journal*, *The Washington Post*, *Salon*, *Politico*, *Time Magazine*, CNN.com, and other nationally prominent places. I wrote on the same metaphysical topics. I made no compromises. I didn't sacrifice my ideals. I didn't cop to an attitude of disbelief, because I am proud to write as a believing historian. Just entering a sense of higher self-capacity, of greater opportunities beyond the artificial boundaries I had constructed, opened things up.

That is why I say that change can occur quickly. Sometimes a mental block can be lowered and you have unified psyche whereas before you were in pieces. All it took was for a thoughtful friend to utter a clarifying sentence. It lifted my blinders. What would lift your blinders? What would give you the ability to reach for your highest ideals? Whatever your field, there is a bottom, middle, and top. Why not fill the needs that place you at the top?

Do you realize that you can live in a larger neighborhood metaphysically and practically? Are you doing things that keep you from that place? Once first causes are identified, the block can lift.

As noted earlier, traditional psychology is right—*but it is not right enough.* Traditional psychology can help you identify first causes but the *removal* of those causes requires the greater powers of your subconscious. Identify what blocks you—do so bravely and without embarrassment. Act as though it is impossible to fail. I guarantee you will step into a vast new territory.

CHAPTER FIVE

Imagination Is More Powerful than Will

At times you may wonder whether it is even necessary to use the higher powers I'm describing. Or whether they are even real. We often hear that all life requires is a clear sense of purpose and a willingness to act. That is, of course, important. We live in a world of action. But there is a final, crucial reason why you must cultivate the powers of your subconscious. It has to do with willpower versus imagination.

Imagination is more powerful than will. Your mental pictures and assumptions matter more than determination. If willpower alone were sufficient to win at the game of life, there would be would be no compulsive behaviors, no intrusive thoughts, and no fecklessness. Your will would be sufficient to overcome these things. But it is not.

French mind theorist Emile Coué, who we met in chapter two, understood the insufficiency of willpower. You will recall that Coué prescribed the famous mantra, "Day by day, in every way, I am getting better and better." By the time of his death in 1926, Coué had thousands of devotees around the world, but he also had many critics. Detractors believed his "day by day" mantra was too childish to solve anything. Yet critics misunderstood that Coué's core insight was not in the words but in *how to use them.*

Coué prescribed gently whispering the affirmation twenty times just before drifting to sleep at night and again just as you are coming to in the morning. He suggested using a knotted string to count off your repetitions, almost like a rosary. That way you don't rouse yourself from semi-slumber. You want the operation to be effortless. Coué recognized the importance of using the recitation during hypnagogia, the period between sleep and wakefulness. The term and concept of hypnagogia did yet not exist in Coué's era but he instinctively grasped its basis. The barrier to affirmations, he realized, is their rejection by your rational mind; Coué offered a work-around. What he prescribed is actually a form of self-hypnosis.

Coué observed that we all have internal blocks. To live self-directed lives we must move beyond these subconscious boundaries. Will-power alone will not accomplish this; it is no match for imagination. To illustrate his point Coué used the following illustration. If you lay a wooden plank on the floor and ask someone to walk its length, he'll have no problem. Take the same plank and raise it twenty feet above the ground, and the task becomes frightful. Not because the physical demands are different but because *we imagine falling*. We receive mental-bodily signals and grow nervous, and hence more likely to fall. The physical demand is identical but the *imagined consequence* changes everything. Coué used that as a metaphor for most of what we experience in life. We are ruled by imagination.

The point of hypnagogic self-suggestion, or what Coué called conscious autosuggestion, is to recondition your imagination so that a task that seems daunting can suddenly seem achievable. In most cases it is, in fact, achievable. Remember what William James observed about leaping over a chasm? Side with the *maybe* and you have a reasonable chance. In fact, it is the only way you have a chance.

*   *   *

I said earlier that we tend to conflate thoughts with emotions. But they are very different. Phrases like positive thinking are useful shorthand; I use it myself—but it doesn't quite get at the nature of things. A great teacher put it this way: thought is like steam power; emotion is like nuclear power. Pitted against each other, emotion wins every time.

The power of self-suggestion requires emotion. The master key to the placebo response is hopeful expectancy. Yet within metaphysical culture I don't think we fully consider whether a suffering person is *capable* of cultivating a mood of hopeful expectancy. Sometimes a person is crushed under the burdens of stress, anxiety, or worldly difficulties; at such points cultivating hopeful expectancy can seem impossible, just when it is needed most. During these times you have an escape hatch. It is prayer.

The Power of your Subconscious Mind says a great deal about prayer. The formula for prayer, Murphy writes, appears in a passage from the New Testament as the ideal stated by Christ: "Therefore I say to you, whatever things you ask when you pray, believe that you receive them, and you will have them." (Mark 11:24, NKJV) Murphy, Neville, Florence Scovel

Shinn, and a wide range of New Thought pioneers prescribe that method. But prescribing confident prayer can reinforce the conundrum I just noted: How do you cultivate a sense of receiving when you are in emotional duress? I do not think that formula always presents a workable solution for someone in crisis.

In actuality, there are *many examples of prayer in Scripture.* There are, for example, cases where the patriarchs and matriarchs answer back to God or argue with God. Cain did this. Moses did this. Jonah did this. Abraham did this. Sarah did this when angels told her that she was going to become pregnant well into her advanced years. The matriarchs and patriarchs sometimes bargained with God. Cain objected to God that his punishment was too severe and that if he wandered the earth like a nomad someone would kill him. God amended his punishment and told Cain that he would place a mark of protection on him, so that if anybody laid a hand on him the assailant would suffer many times over. So there is Biblical precedent for praying in different ways.

You don't have to follow anyone's rules, not mine, not Joseph Murphy's, not that of the tradition that you grew up in. There is no wrong method of prayer. Prayer is an escape route when you are in agony, when you feel unable to summon the positive energies that are the royal road to mental creativity.

Whatever your conception of a greater power, you can petition, you can bargain, you can implore, you can fall to your knees. *There is no entry barrier to prayer.* Mother Nature did not play a cruel trick on us whereby we can receive only when in a state of calm expectancy. If that were true, it would mean that someone crushed by grief or anxiety would be *unable* to solicit greater forces. We are not victims of a cosmic joke. Invisible help is never closed off.

One of my favorite books is *Alcoholics Anonymous*. When it was published in 1939, Bill Wilson, the primary writer, made a radical case that you must appeal to a higher power *as you understand it.* (I personally use the term greater force.) Bill emphasized that principle again and again. He rejected language exclusive to any one tradition. Bill's radical ecumenism proved extremely important because it broadened the reach of AA and delivered help to people in crisis. Bill threw away the rulebook. Learn from his example.

Joseph Murphy's work is scripturally based, and I honor that. But your sense of a higher power or greater force is *yours alone*. It can arise from any number of religious traditions or no religion. It can come from the pantheon of gods. There may be an ancient deity—whether Jupiter, Thoth, Minerva, Set, or another—toward whom you feel drawn. Explore that. Our primeval ancestors had a deep and profound understanding of nature, much deeper than our own. I believe they were right when they identified certain energies within the fabric of nature and personified and named them. These became the gods. I believe this remains a wholly valid and dynamic way of reaching out for invisible help.

I further believe that there is no contradiction between praying to a force that we might perceive as outside of ourselves while also understanding the mind as the seat of creative power. Neville used to say, "If I say the word God and you picture something outside yourself, you've missed the mark." But, again, I don't believe that Mother Nature played a trick on us whereby only certain points of orientation permit us to tap invisible powers.

If greater forces exist, there is no contradiction between making a mental, emotional, spoken or silent appeal to those forces, whether perceived as within or without, or whether experienced in different ways at different times. Concepts of within or without are, in any case, artifice. Life is ultimately whole. "As above, so below." Whether you use the term imagination, subconscious, Yahweh, Jesus,

Jupiter, *there is no barrier*. I mean that very seriously. The spiritual teacher Jiddu Krishnamurti (1885–1886) used to say, "The truth is a pathless land." To assume barriers in how you search is to assume barriers in what you may find.

I am concluding these five lessons with an appeal that you drink from the waters of a wide range of metaphysics. I believe that your own insights and instincts are, finally, the highest and most powerful pathway into the power of your subconscious mind.

The one pertinent measure of a practical philosophy is its impact on conduct. If your belief system supports you in being a more effective, ethical, and generative being, then your personal philosophy would have to be deemed a success.

Write your own book of life. That is what Joseph Murphy did. That is why he attained posterity. He was an individual, like you, who went on a search, discovered principles that proved fortifying, and applied them. I invite you to use his work not as doctrine but as *inspiration*. And you too will peer into the invisible and return with a sense of higher help. When you do, I ask that you not only use it but share it.

AFTERWORD

Posthumous Letters to Joseph Murphy

Several years ago while I was researching the life and work of Joseph Murphy, I came upon a cache of handwritten letters that readers had sent to Murphy's publisher, Prentice Hall, following his death in 1981. The letters originated from places ranging from Nigeria to Sweden to England to Canada to the U.S. Most were dated from the early 1990s.

An editorial assistant plaintively replied to many of these readers, "We regret to inform you that Dr. Joseph Murphy is deceased. Prentice Hall was notified of this in January, 1983." The editorial assistant attempted small acts of kindness, like sending one writer a Spanish-language edition of Murphy's 1968 book, *The Cosmic Power Within You*.

Many of these readers had burning questions. It saddened me to encounter the needs of readers and seekers who were reaching out to a man no longer alive to reply. I hope that by reproducing a selection of these letters and responding as I am able will prove helpful to seekers today who face similar needs. I have indicated locales and dates but omitted names to protect privacy.

November 19, 1992
Stafford, Arizona

Dear Dr. Murphy,

My name is _____. I am 43 years of age. I work in sales and represent three companies in Mexico, and I have my future ahead of me. Only lately I have been real depressed. My girl-friend just left me and I cannot give her up. I love her a lot.

I am reading your book *The Power of Your Subconscious Mind*. And I just think that you can help me overcome this. I wish I could go to one your studies, but if you can send me some literature or what to send for I'll appreciate it.

Answer back soon. I need some help.

Thank you,

_____

Dear _____,

I am sorry to hear you are going through that. I know that experiencing a loss of love can seem like a hole that can never be filled. But I absolutely promise that we very often find solutions in unexpected ways.

It is human nature—and I have experienced it myself—to believe that just one person can fill the needs that we feel. But I refer you to section in this book in which we consider the importance of seeking a *condition* rather than a person or a thing. The condition you seek is love and companionship. I ask you to you to focus on that aim, using the visualizations and exercises in *The Power of Your Subconscious Mind*. I believe that what you need will reach you—perhaps in ways that are more fulfilling than anything you have imagined.

None of us wants to hear that the person on whom we are focused may not be the right one. We rarely believe that when hearing it. But the other person is a complex being with his or her own needs and moral universe. You must allow that person self-expressiveness, just as you wish the same.

Again, focus on the condition and not on one exclusive solution. And I believe that you will find your life moving in the right direction—and you will find someone new.

I am wishing you all good things.

Your friend,
Mitch

March 22, 1991
Surrey, England

Dear Mr. Murphy,

I am writing this letter after reading your excellent book *The Wisdom of Subconscious Mind* [sic].

The purpose of writing this letter is to ask a big favor of you.

For a long time, 10 years, I have had a strong desire which I cannot get out of my mind. It is a good desire which will help me, my family, and other mankind.

I was wondering if you would be kind enough to pray with me, as I am actively praying according to your book's instructions for the fulfillment of this desire. I understand that you are a very busy man and if this is not possible, then do not worry.

Many thanks,

_____

P.S. Please let me know when you are lecturing in England again

Dear _____,

I would be honored to pray with you. I actually maintain a silent prayer group around the world each day at 3 p.m. eastern time. At that time we briefly pause to hold in mind one other's aims and wishes. I call it The Miracle Club. I will be thinking of you then, and invite you to join us.

Wishing you all good things,
Mitch

August 12, 1993
Tampa, Florida

Dear Dr. Murphy,

I keep reading your book *Your Infinite Power to Be Rich* so much that it is falling apart and I still haven't reached my goal of receiving abundance.

I feel that I must be doing something wrong so that I can't break this poverty syndrome. I keep saying these wonderful affirmations but I think I neutralize them because I don't believe I deserve wealth of any kind.

I would like to be financially secure so that I never have to worry about money again. I would like good, supportive relationships and a soul mate.

Somehow I got the impression from my youth that I didn't deserve anything because I'm no good.

Please help me to get out of my poverty.

Sincerely,

_____

Dear _____,

First of all I want to assure you of something—and I want you to remember this for the rest of your life: You are not only good—you are exceptional. This is for the simple fact that you have taken steps that so few people ever consider: striving to heighten your place in life, engaging in inner development, and caring enough about such things to take the time to write a letter to an author whose work touched you. Most people never write one letter in their lives. Most never read a single book, or attend a single lecture, with the aim of raising their sense of self-potential. So, please, let us lay that childhood myth immediately to rest. You are exceptional.

Sometimes saying an affirmation—even with depth of feeling—is not enough. The most remarkable people in recent history, from Helen Keller to Nelson Mandela, led lives of devotion and *action*. They were ardently committed to affecting things in the world. Whatever your employment, throw yourself into it with passion. Be the problem-solver to whom others look for help and advisement. Know more about your job than everyone else, not in a know-it-all way but with the aim of providing service and doing your personal best. Expect—and respectfully require—good wages for your good work. Join a union if you are able and support activists and leaders who defend the rights of workers. But, above all, be the person upon whom all others rely.

Author James Allen was a working-class Englishman who rose from a childhood of poverty to a writing career, largely through his dignity of character and his intelligent persistence. I urge you to read his *As a Man Thinketh*. And when you do, remember that his words and ideas were not the work of someone famous or wealthy. They came from a working person who had tested them in the laboratory of his own life. Also please read Napoleon Hill's *Think and Grow Rich*, which is useful because it combines a program of mental metaphysics with a plan of action.

As for good relationships and finding a soul mate, my counsel is to associate only with people who are supportive and respectful of your search for self-betterment and spiritual awareness. Seek out people who are engaged, in whatever way, in bettering themselves. Spend no time—or as little time as possible—among cynics, bullies, or unproductive people. Avoid those who gossip, and refuse to listen to rumors or hearsay. (Nothing is more deleterious of our relationships or sense of self-respect than engaging in gossip.) Do this, and you will naturally come into the company of true friends and, hopefully, a soul mate.

Your friend,
Mitch

[NOTE: I have transcribed the following letter exactly as it was written, allowing for a slight language barrier but wishing to fully capture this heartfelt note.]

September 13, 1991
Anambra State, Nigeria

Dear Joseph Murphy,
I have the ability to extend my wish to you. I hope by God's power you are normal. It was last week ago a friend of mine gave me your address, then I make up my mind to write you. If you would try as much as possible to

help me in prayer that I have been tormented by the devil-spirit, so I want you to pray for me and cast it away from me and also send me holy books and other things. Furthermore, I am a new person in Christ. So I want you to be my best friend in Christ.

Moreover, I have nothing at all such as a friend. Now I decided to take you as my best friend indeed.

I would be very grateful and thankful to you if you should post me my request. May almighty God be with you. I pray for you that you will post it for me as a brother in Christ.

Reply me please!

Yours faithfully,

_____

Dear _____,

I am honored for you to consider me a friend. I reach to you across the distance that separates us to offer my warm thanks and deepest wishes.

I want you to rest assured that you are not possessed by a devil-spirit or any maleficent spirit. I believe that humanity has misread and misunderstood some of the ancient Biblical parables about serpents, or devils. In many ways the serpent in the Bible was a rebel and emancipator—traits that are necessary to human development. Without friction we can never be truly creative or free.

You are a being who determines his own course. Nothing and no one determines it for you.

I am touched by your note and wish you every good thing in your search.

Your friend—always,
Mitch

July 14, 1991
Quebec, Canada

Dear Dr. Murphy,

I have just finished reading your book entitled "The Cosmic Power Within You" and I found it really interesting. It gave me back hope in life and in my life. Realizing the cosmic powers of god within me and reinforcing my faith in the good things of life have already changed by attitude and gave me a more positive outlook towards life. I am an artist, an oil painter and sometimes it is very hard for me to keep on thinking positive. But this time I decided things are going to change and that I am going to improve my lifestyle. I took the decision and I am positively sure, from now on life is going to be beautiful.

Once again thank you and please accept this reproduction of my painting called "The artist on the street" as a gift expressing my gratitude.

_____

Dear _____,

Thank you for your lovely note. The Hermetic maxim, "As above, so below," repeats in Scripture as, "God created man in his own image." If one takes that principle seriously then it follows that the highest function of the individual is to create, generate, and produce. You are doing this and living out your highest birthright. May you serve as an example to others.

Wishing you all good things,
Mitch

1991 (month unknown)
Billdal, Sweden

Dear Mr. Murphy,
First of all I want to thank you so much! I've just read your book: Miracle of Mind Dynam-

ics and I feel that it has given me so much! Every word seems so right to me. I read a few pages every night before I go to sleep. I don't want to read too much at a time, since there are so many things to learn and think about on every page and besides I want something left to read.

Every since I was young I've felt that God has done a lot of miracles for me, but since I read the book my days are bordered with miracles. I am deeply grateful and I try to show God's love to the people I meet.

There is just one thing I cannot understand and that is why me? I mean I'm no better, nor worse than anyone else. Why so much love to me? Why are children hurt, tortured and killed. Why do so many have to starve. Are they more evil? They must also be loved by God since they too are his children.

This is so hard for me to understand—and I would so much want an explanation . . .

Lots of love,

_____

Dear _____,

Thank you for your thoughtful and honest note. You pose the most sensitive question in mind metaphysics: *why me?* This question can be asked in the negative or in the positive, as you have.

I am responding to your long-ago letter during the first weeks of the 2020 pandemic that has gripped the world and, in particular, my city of New York. I write you quarantined in my apartment on the Lower East Side, nearing week three of my own (thankfully mild) bout with coronavirus.

Joseph Murphy wrote about the impact of accumulated thought—of parents sometimes passing down thought forms to a child. He further theorized that the cumulative thoughts of humanity, extending to deep antiquity, can outpicture in our present world and in the physical life of an individual.

I accept neither of those views.

If we surmise that all the thoughts that have ever been can outpicture and cause suffering in the physical life of someone today, we more or less accept the premise of randomness, since vast and unknowable thoughts have occurred for thousands of years. Randomness contradicts the rest of Murphy's system and the purpose of New Thought in general.

If we propose that the thoughts of a parent can be visited upon a child, and can result, apropos of your concerns, in profound physical suffering or illness, I also reject that cause and effect.

I have witnessed circumstances, as I am sure you have, of a child suffering and dying from chronic disease in an atmosphere of love and support. Pointing to a parent (a ghastly proposition), or pointing to a thinker or thinkers in antiquity, seems like an effort to plug a philosophical gap rather than respond meaningfully to suffering.

Matters get more troublesome when New Thought tries to explain chronic tragedies or catastrophes by appending ideas of karma onto positive-thinking philosophy. Past-life sins, in this view, could explain why a person, or millions of people, experience painful lives or violent deaths. Such reasoning appeared in the late 1950s in the work of a widely read metaphysical writer, Gina Cerminara. Cerminara had previously done a great deal to popularize the work of the psychic Edgar Cayce in her 1950 book, *Many Mansions*. In a later book, *The World Within,* Cerminara attempted to bring a karmic perspective to global suffering. "Present-day Negroes," she suggested in 1957, might understand the roots of their racial oppression if they

> *can project themselves back into the past and in imagination see themselves to be brutal English slavetraders, arrogant Virginia slaveholders, or conscienceless Ala-*

bama auctioneers, smugly assured of their white supremacy—if they can make this imaginative leap, their own present situation may seem far more intelligible and far more bearable.

Her advice continued:

Present-day Jews who feel that they are the victims of unjust prejudice should reflect that a long racial history of regarding themselves as a "chosen people," and of practicing racial exclusiveness and pride, cannot but lead to a situation where they themselves will be excluded.

Such arguments collapse under any degree of ethical scrutiny. Spiritual insight arrives through *self-observation*—not justifying the suffering experienced *by another.* To judge others is to work without any self-verification, which is the key empirical tool of the spiritual search.

The private person who can maturely and persuasively claim self-responsibility for *his own* suffering, or endure it as an inner obligation, shines a light for others. The person who justifies *someone else's* suffering, such as through collective fault, only casts a stone.

Retrofitting current spiritual or ethical conundrums onto the ancient philosophy of karma, a vast and complex thought system, is almost admitting that one's chosen outlook doesn't work. Yet I believe that New Thought or mind-metaphysics *does* work. As a seeker, I believe that thoughts are causative.

So why do we witness mass suffering in a purportedly self-created mental universe?

I venture that we live under and experience many laws and forces. Physical decline and mortality alone tell us that. Although I believe, like my intellectual hero Neville Goddard, that mind is the ultimate arbiter of reality, its effects are mitigated by circumstance.

A law, in order to be a law, must be ever operative. The law of gravity is ever operative. But you are going to experience radically different effects from gravity on earth than on the moon or Jupiter. In the vacuum of space gravity appears absent. Introduce mass into the cosmic vacuum and gravity is felt. Gravity is, in a sense, mass being attracted to itself. Hence, natural laws are conditioned by circumstance. I see the law of mental creativity no differently.

A child who is born into circumstances of war, disease, natural disaster, violence, or poverty faces crushing (and socially reinforced) mitigating factors. Thought is one powerful vehicle among others in the possession of the individual. Thought has, I believe, causative properties, as I have argued widely. But we must never harbor the illusion of an equal playing field, geographically, socially, physically, or politically. Until New Thought allows for the experience of multiple laws and forces within our physical framework (a topic well handled in the 1908 book *The Kybalion* and in classical Hermetic literature) the field of mind metaphysics will fail to deal maturely with suffering.

Suffering is inevitable. Life, by its very nature, is cyclical. "As above, so below." That principle does not abrogate the philosophy of mind causation. But it must affect it. New Thought's acolytes, if they are theologically serious, must persuasively respond to suffering. In that vein, I offer you the words of Rabbi Joshua Loth Liebman (1907–1948), one of the few leaders in the positive-mind movement who directly addressed the Holocaust. Two years after the war, the Boston rabbi said:

Mine has been a rabbinate of trouble—of depression. Hitler's rise, world crisis, global war, the attempted extermination of my people . . . For those who have lost loved ones during the tragic war, all of the rest of life will be but a half loaf of bread—yet a half loaf eaten in courage and accepted in truth is infinitely better than a moldy whole loaf, green with the decay of self-pity and selfish sorrow which really dishonors the memory of those who lived for our up building and happiness.

We honor life by valuing the sacrifices that others have made for us, and the opportunities we are granted for developing our highest potential.

Philosopher Jacob Needleman once asked me: "What do you do when someone offers you a gift?" After I looked at him blankly, he replied: "You accept it." The continuation of one's life following a tragedy is to accept an irreplaceable gift. We have been given life for a purpose, which is: to be *generative*. Use your life. Go and build.

Your friend,
Mitch

Joseph Murphy
Timeline

This timeline is intended as a resource for writers, seekers, and students of Joseph Murphy and of the American metaphysical tradition in general. It is also intended as a corrective to some of the misinformation that has circulated about Murphy, such as his studying with Swami Vivekananda (1863–1902), English judge and mystic Thomas Troward (1847–1916)—both of whom lived and worked at disparate times and distances from Murphy—or dubious details about his childhood home and educational background. This timeline represents the most complete information that I could locate through immigration records, Murphy's few interviews, and cross-referenced sources.

1898—Joseph Denis Murphy is born on May 20, the fourth of five children (three girls and two boys) to a devout Catholic family on the Southern Coast of Ireland in Ballydehob, County Cork. Murphy's father was headmaster of a local boys high school.

Circa 1914–1915—After being educated locally, Murphy studies chemistry in Dublin. Bowing to his parents' wishes he enrolls briefly in a Jesuit seminary. Dissatisfied with his studies, and unbelieving of the doctrine of no salvation outside the church, Murphy leaves seminary.

Circa 1916–1918—Murphy works as a pharmacist for England's Royal Army Medical Corps during World War I.

1918-1921—Murphy works as a in pharmacist in Dublin. He earns a monthly salary of about $10.

1922—Dissatisfied with traditional religion and finding limited opportunities to practice as a chemist, Murphy just shy of age 24 arrives in New York City on April 17, 1922. He is accompanied by his wife, Madolyn, who is eight years his senior (wedding date unknown). He arrives with $23. Applies for citizenship in August.

1923–1938—Murphy works as a pharmacist in New York City including at a pharmacy counter at the Algonquin Hotel. He deepens his study into metaphysics and years later recounts having studied with the figure of Abdullah, a black man of Jewish descent whom Murphy's contemporary and fellow New Yorker, Neville Goddard (1905–1972), wrote that he studied with. Murphy reports that Abdullah tells Murphy that he actually had three brothers, not two. Upon checking with his mother, Murphy discovers that he had a third brother who died at birth and was never spoken of.

Circa 1931—Murphy begins attending the Church of the Healing Christ in New York City, presided over by Emmet Fox.

Circa 1938—Murphy is ordained as a Divine Science minster. He continues to work as a druggist and chemist.

1941—Murphy begins broadcasting metaphysical sermons over the radio.

1942—Murphy enlists as a pharmacist in the New York State National Guard, a post he holds until 1948.

1943—Murphy studies Tarot in New York City and comes to believe in symbolic correspondences between the Tarot cards and Scripture.

1945—Murphy writes his first book, *This Is It: The Art Of Metaphysical Demonstration.*

1946—Murphy is ordained as a Religious Science Minister in Los Angeles. He soon takes over the pulpit of the Institute for Religious Science in Rochester, New York. He publishes the short works *Wheels of Truth, The Perfect Answer,* and *Fear Not.*

1948—Murphy publishes *St. John Speaks, Love is Freedom,* and *The Twelve Powers Mystically Explained.*

1949—Murphy is re-ordained into Divine Science and becomes minister of the Los Angeles Divine Science Church, a post he will hold for the next 28 years. Services become so popular that they are held at the Wilshire Ebell Theater.

1952—Publishes *Riches Are Your Right.*

1953—Publishes *The Miracles of Your Mind, The Fragrance of God,* and *How to Use the Power of Prayer.*

1954—Publishes *The Magic of Faith* and *The Meaning of Reincarnation*, one of his most controversial books.

1955—Publishes *Believe in Yourself* and *How to Attract Money*, one of his most enduringly popular works.

1956—Murphy writes *Traveling With God* in which he recounts his international speaking tours, comparing New Thought with various global traditions. He also publishes *Peace Within Yourself* (*St. John Speaks* revised) and *Prayer Is the Answer*.

1957—Publishes *How to Use Your Healing Power.*

1958—Publishes the short works *Quiet Moments with God, Pray Your Way Through It, The Healing Power of Love, Stay Young Forever, Mental Poisons and Their Antidotes,* and *How to Pray With a Deck of Cards.*

1959—Publishes *Living Without Strain.*

1960—Publishes *Techniques in Prayer Therapy.*

1961—Publishes *You Can Change Your Whole Life* and *Nuclear Religion.*

1962—Publishes *Why Did This Happen to Me?*

1963—Publishes *The Power of Your Subconscious Mind,* which becomes a worldwide bestseller and a landmark of New Thought philosophy. The book's publication makes Murphy into one of the most widely known metaphysical writers in the world.

1964—Publishes *The Miracle of Mind Dynamics.*

1965—Publishes *The Amazing Laws of Cosmic Mind Power.*

1966—Publishes *Your Infinite Power to Be Rich.*

1968—Publishes *The Cosmic Power Within You.*

1969—Publishes *Infinite Power for Richer Living.*

1970—Publishes *Secrets of the I Ching.*

1971—Publishes *Psychic Perception: The Magic of Extrasensory Perception.*

1972—Publishes *Miracle Power for Infinite Riches*

1973—Publishes *Telepsychics: The Magic Power of Perfect Living* (1973)

1974—Publishes *The Cosmic Energizer: Miracle Power of the Universe* (1974)

1976—Murphy's first wife Madolyn dies. He remarries his secretary, Jean L. Murphy (nee Wright), also a Divine Science minister. He writes *Great Bible Truths for Human Problems.*

1977—Publishes *Within You Is the Power*

1979—Publishes *Songs of God*

1980—Publishes *How to Use the Laws of Mind*

1981—Murphy dies on December 16 in Laguna Hills, CA, where he and his wife Jean are living at the Leisure World retirement community, now known as Laguna Woods Village.

1982—*These Truths Can Change Your Life* is published posthumously.

1987—Canadian writer Bernard Cantin publishes the French language work *Joseph Murphy se raconte à Bernard Cantin* [*Joseph Murphy Speaks to Bernard Cantin*] with Quebec's Éditions Un Monde Différent. The book is based on an extended series of interviews Cantin conducted with Murphy before his death and provides a rare window into Murphy's career. It does not appear in English. *The Collected Essays of Joseph Murphy* is published posthumously.

About the Author

Mitch Horowitz is a historian of alternative spirituality and one of today's most literate voices of esoterica, mysticism, and the occult.

He is widely credited with returning the term "New Age" to respectable use and is among the few occult writers whose work touches the bases of academic scholarship, national journalism, and subculture cred.

Mitch is a 2020 writer-in-residence at the New York Public Library, lecturer-in-residence at the Philosophical Research Society in Los Angeles, and the PEN Award-winning author of books including *Occult America; One Simple Idea: How Positive Thinking Reshaped Modern Life; The Miracle Club*; and *The Miracle Habits.*

He has discussed alternative spirituality on CBS Sunday Morning, Dateline NBC, Vox/

Netflix's *Explained*, and Shudder's *Cursed Films*, an official selection of SXSW 2020. Mitch is collaborating with director Ronni Thomas (Tribeca Film Festival) on a feature documentary about the occult classic *The Kybalion*, shot on location in Egypt.

Mitch has written on everything from the war on witches to the secret life of Ronald Reagan for *The New York Times*, *The Wall Street Journal*, *The Washington Post*, *Time*, *Politico*, and a wide range of 'zines and scholarly journals. He narrates audio books including *Alcoholics Anonymous* and *Raven: The Untold Story of the Rev. Jim Jones and His People* (the author of which handpicked him as the voice of Jones).

Mitch received the 2019 Walden Award for Interfaith/Intercultural Understanding. The Chinese government has censored his work.

Printed in the USA
CPSIA information can be obtained
at www.ICGtesting.com
JSHW012042140824
68134JS00033B/3217

9 781722 501723